Learning to Listen, Learning to Care

A Workbook to Help Kids Learn Self-Control & Empathy

LAWRENCE E. SHAPIRO, PH.D.

Instant Help Books
A Division of New Harbinger Publications, Inc.

Publisher's Note

Distributed in Canada by Raincoast Books

Copyright © 2008 by Lawrence Shapiro
          Instant Help Books
          A Division of New Harbinger Publications, Inc.
          5674 Shattuck Avenue
          Oakland, CA 94609
          www.newharbinger.com

Cover design by Amy Shoup

Library of Congress Cataloging-in-Publication Data

Shapiro, Lawrence E.
  Learning to listen, learning to care : a workbook to help kids learn empathy and self-control / by Lawrence E. Shapiro.
    p. cm.
  ISBN-13: 978-1-57224-598-3 (pbk. : alk. paper)
  ISBN-10: 1-57224-598-0 (pbk. : alk. paper)
 1. Empathy--Study and teaching.--Activity programs. 2. Self-control in children--Study and teaching--Activity programs. I. Title.
  BF575.E55S45 2008
  177'.7--dc22

                        2007051959

10   09   08

10   9   8   7   6   5   4   3   2   1

Table of Contents

A Note to Parents

Many children today have behavioral problems. They may have mild problems such as talking back or being uncooperative, or they may have more serious problems like throwing tantrums or hitting other children.

You have probably heard or read the standard advice on getting kids to behave. There are basic principles to parenting children with behavioral problems, including:

- Understand the reasons why your child is misbehaving.

- Have consistent rules and age-appropriate expectations for your child.

- Reward good behavior with praise or a point system.

- Be a good role model.

- Provide appropriate discipline for misbehavior (such as time-outs or taking away privileges).

These principles will always apply, but this workbook adds a new approach to helping children with behavioral problems. The activities in this workbook will help you teach your children the emotional, social, and behavioral skills they need to be kinder, more considerate, and more cooperative.

The activities in this workbook are very similar to the ones that a counselor would use to help children overcome behavior problems. They will help your child manage his anger, develop a better understanding of others, see the value of helping and caring, and much more. Each activity teaches your child a new emotional intelligence skill, and once learned, these skills will not only improve his behavior at home, they will also help him make new friends and develop the habits that lead to school and work success.

Children learn emotional intelligence skills just like they learn academic or athletic skills: through practice and encouragement. Your child will likely need your guidance going through this workbook, and he or she will certainly need your encouragement.

As you help your child, you will probably find out that it is difficult for him to talk about certain issues. Never force your child to talk if he doesn't want to. The best way to get children to open up is to be a good role model. Talk about your thoughts, feelings, and experiences as they relate to each activity, stressing the positive ways that *you* cope with problems. Even if your child doesn't say a thing back, your words will have an impact on his behavior.

This workbook was designed to help any child with behavioral problems, but your child may need some additional help as well. There are many reasons why children misbehave, and a thorough evaluation will help you pinpoint just what needs to be done. If you are concerned about your child's behavior, I urge you to get help soon. Misbehavior attracts negative responses from the people around your child, which then leads to more misbehavior. The sooner that you break this cycle of negativity, the easier it will be for your child to learn new, positive behaviors. If your child needs professional help—or if you need some guidance—you will find this workbook to be of added benefit. Show it to your counselor, and she may have some additional ideas on the best way to use it.

There is no wrong way to use this workbook as long as you remain patient and respectful of your child's feelings. Parenting can have its difficult moments, but I hope that the positive approaches to difficult behaviors in this book will help.

Sincerely,

Lawrence Shapiro, Ph.D.

A Note to Kids

Dear Reader,

I bet that you have people telling you how they want you to behave all of the time. I also bet that they might not be telling you to behave in ways that you want to hear.

Do your parents yell at you? Do you get punished for not doing what they want you to? Do your teachers give you a hard time? Do you ever have to stay after school or go to the principal's office? Do your friends get mad at you? Do you sometimes wish that everyone would just leave you alone?

If you have answered "yes" to any of these questions, this book can help you.

This is a book about learning to do the things that will make everyone who is giving you a hard time feel better about how you behave. It is a book about learning to behave in ways that will bring you closer to people and make you feel better about yourself.

Now you might think that it's not your fault that other people give you a hard time, that it is really their problem, not yours. The truth is that when people are unhappy with each other, it is everyone's problem. Another truth is that you can't change anyone else's behavior, but you can change yours. And changing your behavior is what this book is about.

I also hope that you will find most of the activities in this book fun. Changing your behavior is not easy to do, but I hope that this book will make it a little easier.

Good luck!

Lawrence Shapiro, Ph.D.

> ## *For You to Know*
>
> Talking about how you feel is an important part of getting along with others.

We all want other people, particularly our parents, to understand our feelings and to act in the ways we want.

For example, Johnny had a terrible day in school. He got into a fight with Arthur, his teacher yelled at him, and he got a poor grade on his book report. When he came home, his mother was happy to see him, and she gave him a hug and said, "Hi, Honey, would you like some brownies that I just made?"

But Johnny was in such a bad mood that he didn't want to be hugged, and he didn't want a brownie, and his mother's cheerfulness irritated him.

He yelled at her: "Can't you just leave me alone!"

Johnny's mother was very surprised at his reaction, and she was hurt. Then she got mad, too. She said, "Okay, if you want to be that way, then just go to your room."

Johnny went to his room, and now he was mad at his mother, too! Both Johnny and his mother stayed mad for the rest of the evening.

Things would have gone much better if Johnny just said, "I'm in a bad mood because I had a bad day." Then his mother would have known why he was acting that way, and she might have even asked him to talk about his bad mood. Johnny would probably have felt much better if he had talked about his bad day.

Your challenge: Start talking about your feelings rather than just expecting people to read your mind.

For You to Do

Many children find it easier to express their feelings by drawing them. Then they can talk about what they drew. In the space below, draw a picture of how you are feeling right now. Then talk about what made you feel this way.

...And More to Do!

What are three things that always make you happy?

1. _____

2. _____

3. _____

What are three things that always make you mad?

1. _____

2. _____

3. _____

Who do you think you can talk to about your feelings?

_____

_____

_____

What can you do to create a time and place to talk about your feelings?

_____

_____

_____

_____

Dealing with Difficult Feelings

> ## For You to Know
>
> Everyone has many different feelings. Some feelings are harder to talk about than others. When you understand your different feelings, you will find it easier to get along with others.

Your feelings are changing all of the time, even though you may not be aware of it. Every day you have many feelings, and some of them, like anger or sadness or guilt, may cause you to behave in ways that just make things worse. Talking about your feelings will usually help you find ways to cope with difficult feelings and difficult situations. But sometimes it is hard to talk about or even think about what you are feeling. For example:

- You might be sad because a pet died.

- You might be afraid of dogs, but you don't want your friends to know it.

- You might have lied, and you feel guilty about it.

- You might be angry because a parent yelled at you for no good reason.

Even though it is hard, it is important to think about and talk about your difficult feelings.

- When you talk about these feelings, you will feel better.

- When you talk about these feelings, people will understand you better and may even behave differently toward you.

- There are many positive and creative ways to deal with difficult feelings. to cope with your difficult feelings is an important part of growing up.

Your challenge: If you are upset or feeling bad, take time to think about why you are feeling this way and what you can do about it.

For You to Do

Look at the pictures of the kids with the different feelings. Write down the most recent time that you had each of these feelings.

Happy

Angry

_____

_____

_____

Sad

Worried

...And More to Do!

What is the feeling that you have most often?

_____

_____

_____

What is a feeling that you almost never have?

_____

_____

_____

Do you ever have two different feelings at the same time? Describe a situation where you might have two different feelings at the same time.

_____

_____

_____

How are you feeling right now? What do you think is making you feel this way?

_____

_____

_____

_____

Listening to the Feelings of Others

For You to Know

When you listen to the feelings of others in a respectful way, people will like you better and treat you better.

Many people don't know how to listen in a good way when others are talking. Even adults sometimes think that they are good listeners, but they are not.

To be a good listener, you have to:

- Look at the other person when they are speaking.

- Not interrupt.

- Let the other person know that you care about what they are talking about.

There are many ways to let someone know that you care about what they are talking about. The easiest thing to do is to ask questions about what they are saying. It is also important to have "body language" (see Activity #4) that shows you are listening. If you are doing something else, or if you are turned away from the person who is speaking, they will not think that you care about what they have to say.

Are you a good listener? If not, this is something you should learn. I guarantee that if you work on being a good listener you will get along better with everyone in your life—your parents, your teachers, and your friends.

Your challenge: Really think about what you are doing when other people are talking to you, and show them that you are listening to what they are saying.

For You to Do

It is important to practice good listening habits. Ask a parent or another adult to practice with you.

Ask the person any of the following questions:

What is something you love to do?

What was the best trip you ever took?

What happened to you recently that you will never forget?

What is your best memory from when you were little?

Practice making eye contact, not interrupting, and asking questions that show your interest. Now ask that person to rate you below, on a 1 to 10 scale. 1 = Poor, 10 = Great.

_____ You really looked as if you were listening to me.

_____ You didn't interrupt me.

_____ You asked good questions.

_____ You made me feel like you cared about what I was saying.

Total score _____

...And More to Do!

Practice your listening skills once a day. Think of five people you can practice these listening skills on without telling them what you are doing.

How will you know if your better listening skills are making a difference?

_____

_____

_____

_____

Who do you know that you would call a "good listener"? Why did you choose that person?

_____

_____

_____

_____

How do you think that things might change in your life when you become a good listener?

_____

_____

_____

_____

Activity 4   Reading Body Language

> ## For You to Know
>
> Nonverbal language, or body language, speaks louder than your words.

When you want to say something to someone, you probably just open your mouth and say it. But your nonverbal language, your body language, also says a lot. Your body language consists of your facial expression, your posture (how you stand or sit), your gestures, and more. Even what you wear or your hygiene is part of your nonverbal language. Being aware of your nonverbal language is important in relating to others.

It is important to be aware of your own body language (see Activity #5) as well as the body language of others.

When you know how to read the body language of others, you will be able to understand their feelings more easily.

It's also really cool to be able to read body language. Police men and women read body language to see if someone is lying. Teachers read the body language of their students to see if they are paying attention. Card players and chess players read body language to try and understand their opponents.

Your challenge: You can learn to read the body language of other people to understand how they are really feeling.

For You to Do

In this assignment you will learn to pay attention to what other people are saying with their body language.

Look at the gestures below. What does each of them mean? Think of 10 other common gestures that people you know use all of the time.

_____

_____

_____

_____

_____

_____

Other Gestures

_____

_____

_____

_____

_____

_____

...And More to Do!

Who do you know who has body language that is very easy to read? What are some of the things that they do?

_____

_____

_____

What are some gestures that people use to show that they approve of something you did?

_____

_____

_____

Describe how a person's face and body might look if they were sad.

_____

_____

_____

Describe how a person's face and body might look if they were afraid.

_____

_____

_____

Speaking with Positive Body Language

> ## *For You to Know*
>
> Body language is an important way of expressing your feelings. If you use positive body language when you speak to others, they will be more likely to respond in a positive way.

When you speak to other people, they are not only listening to what you say but also are looking at how you say it. They are watching your posture, your facial expression, your gestures, and so on. People who are leaders, whether they are the kids in your class or the politicians who run our country, almost always use positive body language when you talk to others.

Positive body language involves having a confident posture, making eye contact with people, and using gestures to get your meaning across. In this exercise, you should practice using positive body language.

Stand in front of a mirror, and take a pose that shows you are confident and happy.

- Stand straight.

- Look yourself in the eyes.

- Smile.

- Now make a gesture that is friendly.

- Hold out your hand as if you were going to shake someone's hand.

- Wave "hi" to yourself.

Your challenge: Use positive body language with people when discussing something important.

For You to Do

Cut out magazine pictures of people with positive body language. This could include facial expression, posture, gestures, or all of these. Use additional paper if you need to, and show as many types of positive body language as you can.

...And More to Do!

How can use your body language to get someone's attention in a good way?

_____

_____

_____

How do people use their body language to get attention in a negative way?

_____

_____

_____

Everyone likes people who smile. How many times do you think you smile in a day?
What is another positive way you use your body language during the day?

_____

_____

_____

Think of the kids in your class. Which ones do you think have positive body language?
What do you think about these kids?

_____

_____

_____

Activity 6

The Mean Face vs. the Smiling Face

For You to Know

Your facial expression is an important way that you communicate your feelings to others. It is part of your nonverbal language, and it is even more important than your words. If you give angry or mean looks to people who care about you or to people who are trying to help you, it is just as bad as yelling at them or acting mean.

Have you ever noticed that some people seem to smile a lot and some people seem to frown a lot and always look unhappy? Whom would you rather be around, someone who looks happy most of the time or someone who looks unhappy most of the time?

 You should think about how you look to others. Do you look unhappy or angry most of the time, or do you look pleasant and positive most of the time? When a parent or teacher asks you to do something, do you give them a mean or angry face, or do you have a positive expression on your face?

I guarantee you that if you practice having a more positive expression on your face—particularly when someone asks you to do something—adults will treat you better and kids will want to be with you.

Your challenge: Try being more aware of the expression on your face. When an adult talks to you, try and smile and look the adult in the eye. See if this makes a difference in the way that people treat you.

For You to Do

Ask someone to take a picture of you while you are smiling. Take several pictures and try to really look like you are sincerely happy. Paste the picture in the space below.

Now have someone ask you the questions below. Try and keep a smiling face and a pleasant attitude as you say, "Okay, I'll do it," to each question. Then ask that person to rate whether you were able to maintain a pleasant expression while responding to each question. 1 = Positive/pleasant face and 10 = Mean/angry face.

Will you take out the trash? Rating _____

Will you do your homework now? Rating _____

Please get ready for bed. Rating _____

Will you clean up your room? Rating _____

...And More to Do!

Who do you know that makes mean faces a lot?

_____

_____

_____

Who do you know that always has a pleasant expression?

_____

_____

_____

How will you remember that it is important to have a pleasant expression?

_____

_____

_____

When do you think is the one time that it is really important to have a pleasant expression? Why did you choose this time?

_____

_____

_____

For You to Know

If you think that you are in a bad mood a lot of the time, you can do something about it. You can find out the things that put you in a bad mood, and you can try to change them.

Sometimes it is easy to see why someone is in a bad mood. If you have a fight with a friend or you have homework that is really hard, that might put you in a bad mood. Other times it is hard to see why someone is in a bad mood. Some people just seem to be irritable and angry all of the time.

People are born with different personalities. Some people seem to be happy almost all of the time. Some people seem to be unhappy almost all of the time. On a 1 to 10 scale with 1 = Very happy most of the time and 10 = Very unhappy most of the time, where would you rate yourself?

If you gave yourself a rating of "5" or more, you need to learn how to make yourself be in a better mood most of the time.

In this activity, you will keep track of your mood and what happened during that time of the day. Then, see if you can change the things that put you in a bad mood. Be prepared to change things that you might not like. For example, if you are in a bad mood in the morning because your mother yells at you to get up, you can go to bed earlier so that it will be easier to get up. Most kids don't like to go to bed earlier, but consider that this will avoid an argument every morning and will also make you feel more rested.

For You to Do

The first thing that can help you change your unhappy moods is to find out if anything in particular causes them. No one is unhappy all of the time (even if it may seem that way), and probably there are times of day or certain situations that make you feel more unhappy.

Fill in the chart below as often during the day as you can. You can get an adult to help you if you like. Rate your mood with 1 = Very happy and 10 = Very unhappy. Then, think if there is anything you can do to change your unhappy moods.

Time of Day	What Happened	Your Mood	What Can You Change?
8 A.M.			
9 A.M.			
10 A.M.			
11 A.M.			
12 P.M.			
1 P.M.			
2 P.M.			
3 P.M.			
4 P.M.			
5 P.M.			
6 P.M.			
7 P.M.			
8 P.M.			

...And More to Do!

What are some of the things that put you in a bad mood?

_____

_____

_____

Your mood affects other people. Who do you think is most affected when you are in an unhappy mood?

_____

_____

_____

Why should you bother trying to have a more pleasant mood?

_____

_____

_____

Are there certain times of the day that you feel more irritable and unhappy? Is this the same every day of the week?

_____

_____

_____

For You to Know

You don't have to let your feelings control your behavior. You can learn to keep calm, even though you might be angry or upset.

A lot of people aren't able to control their feelings. Not just kids, but grownups too. You might have seen kids lose their tempers when they are frustrated, or grownups that yell and get upset because they are in a traffic jam.

Sometimes you can't help but get angry, but many people get angry so often that other people don't like to be with them.

Do you get angry too often? Do you find yourself losing your temper or being mad almost every day? If this is the case, there are many things that you can do, and you can learn them in the next three activities.

To begin with, you have to know how to keep calm, even when you are frustrated or upset. Even when someone is teasing you. Even when someone annoys you. You can calm yourself down and keep from getting upset almost any time if you really try.

Your challenge: To practice relaxation techniques every day.

Keeping Calm Even Though You Are Upset

For You to Do

Take a pencil and put it on one of the seven Anger Monsters; then slowly, very slowly, move it to the picture of the cage. As you move the pencil, breathe deeply in and out very slowly. It should take you at least 2 minutes to get to the cage. Write down how long it takes you to get to the cage. Even though you are moving your hand, try and relax all of the muscles of your body as you move your pencil. Put another monster in the cage every day for the next week. Write down how long it takes you, seeing if you can increase the time with each monster.

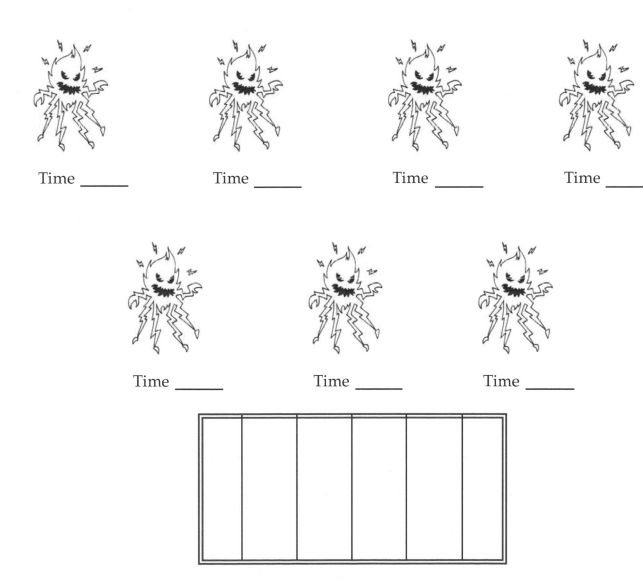

Time _____   Time _____   Time _____   Time _____

Time _____   Time _____   Time _____

...And More to Do!

It is important to practice deep breathing and relaxing your muscles every day. When could you do this?

_____

_____

_____

Among the people you know, who keeps calm, even when there is a lot of stress?

_____

_____

_____

Some people have a secret signal to remind them to calm down when they are upset. A secret signal could be something like tapping the back of your hand or just snapping your fingers. What could be your secret signal?

_____

_____

_____

Who could help you practice your deep breathing and relaxing?

_____

_____

_____

There Are Better and Worse Ways to Show Your Feelings

For You to Know

Your feelings play a big part in what you do. When you get angry you may yell or sulk or even throw something. When you are sad you may sleep more than you usually do, or you may just lie around watching TV. When you are happy, you probably like to play and have fun and be with other people.

There is a part of our brains that controls our emotions. Some of the time that part of the brain tells us things that are good for us to do, and sometimes that part of the brain tells us things that don't help us at all or even hurt others.

But even though the emotional part of your brain may tell you to do something to express a particular feeling, you still have a CHOICE. You can choose the best way to express any of your feelings.

Your challenge: Be aware of your feelings, and recognize that you have a choice about how to express them.

There Are Better and Worse Ways to Show Your Feelings

For You to Do

Circle the better ways to show each of the feelings below.

Angry

Hit a wall.   Talk about what's bothering you.   Spit.

Curse.   Do some exercise.   Yell at the person making you angry.

Think about what is bothering you and try to change things.

Sad

Eat some candy.   Complain to your parents.   Talk to someone.

Think about what is bothering you.   Whine.

Afraid

Stay away from what you are afraid of.   Read about the things you are afraid of.

Talk to someone about how to face your fears.

Sorry

Write a note of apology.   Just forget about what happened.

Happy

Brag about things.   Try and make someone else happy.

Try and always get your own way so you will always be happy.

...And More to Do!

Can you think of a time when you were angry and you behaved in a way that made things worse?

_____

_____

_____

Can you think of a time when you were afraid and you did something to face your fears?

_____

_____

_____

Can you think of a time when you were sad and you did something that made you feel better?

_____

_____

_____

Can you think of a time when you felt sorry about something that you did and you did something to make things right again?

_____

_____

_____

Activity 10 Changing Your Feelings and Behavior Using Self-Talk

For You to Know

Everyone talks to themselves . . . all of the time. Sometimes people call this "self-talk," because you are talking to yourself and not to anyone else. Self-talk can help you have a better attitude about your life and more positive feelings toward others.

Sometimes people say negative things to themselves when they are upset. They may say things like:

"I'm so stupid."

"Nobody likes me."

"Why can't I do anything right!"

This kind of self-talk just makes you feel worse. But you can learn to say things to yourself that will make you feel better! You can say things to yourself that will help you do things that can improve your attitude and even your performance in school and in sports. Many performers and athletes use self-talk to calm themselves down when they are nervous or to encourage themselves when they want to do something difficult.

In this activity, we'll work on using self-talk to have a positive attitude, even when you are facing a difficult task.

Your challenge: Learn to say positive rather than negative things to yourself.

For You to Do

Imagine that you are doing some very difficult homework.

List five things that you could say to yourself that would help you to keep trying with a positive attitude. Here are three examples to get you started.

"I just have to concentrate."

"I can do this."

"Relax and keep working."

1. _____

2. _____

3. _____

4. _____

5. _____

...And More to Do!

Why do you think it's important to have a positive attitude?

_____

_____

_____

_____

What are you thinking right now? Write your thoughts down and determine if they are positive or negative.

_____

_____

_____

_____

_____

_____

_____

_____

_____

_____

> ## *For You to Know*
>
> People feel good when you listen to their feelings. Listening to someone's feelings, even if you don't agree with what they say or understand how they feel, is an important way of showing that you care.

Feelings are an important part of who people are. When you listen to other people talk about their feelings, you show that you are paying attention to them and that you care about them. When you don't listen to their feelings, it is a way of saying, "I don't care."

When you listen to someone's feelings, you can begin to understand them better. This will help you develop good friends and a closer relationship with your parents and teachers.

Some children say, "I don't want friends. I don't care what my parents or teachers or anyone thinks of me." But even when children say this, they are expressing feelings: feelings of anger, feelings of disappointment, maybe even feelings of sadness. Feelings are what connect people to each other, and everyone needs to be connected to other people.

Your challenge: Start asking questions about how other people feel, and listen to what they say without comment or criticism.

For You to Do

Use the form below to have an interview with three different people about their feelings (you will need to make three copies of this page). You can write their answers or you can tape record what they have to say.

Feelings Interview

Name of person being interviewed _____ Date _____

Who is the one person that always cheers you up? _____

What is a book or movie that you think is sad? Why does it make you sad?

_____

_____

What is something you are afraid of but you don't think you should be afraid of?

_____

_____

When you are angry, what do you do to calm yourself down?

_____

_____

What is something you did that you were proud of?

_____

_____

_____

...And More to Do!

Of the three people that you interviewed, who liked talking most about his/her feelings?

_____

Which person used the most expressive body language when talking about his/her feelings?

_____

What new thing did you learn about each of the three people that you interviewed?

_____

_____

_____

_____

On a 1 to 10 scale, how do you rate yourself as a listener (1 = poor, 10 = great)?

poor 1   2   3   4   5   6   7   8   9   10   **great**

What did you learn about your own listening skills?

_____

_____

_____

_____

You Can Change Your Feelings If You Want To

> ## *For You to Know*
>
> Here's a secret that many people don't know: You can change your feelings if you don't like them.

Many people think that their feelings have a tremendous amount of power and that their feelings control their behavior. I know people who are afraid of flying, and they never go on an airplane. I know people who worry about things that they can't control, and they spend a lot of their time worrying about those things.

These people don't know that they can change these difficult feelings, and you can change yours, too.

If you are angry, you can control your anger. If you are frustrated, you can calm yourself down and feel better. If you are unhappy, you can be happier.

In this activity, you will learn some different ways to change your feelings. You should try them all out, and then practice the ones that work best in a situation that often bothers you.

Your challenge: Find ways to make yourself feel happier about your life.

For You to Do

On the next few pages are things that people do to make themselves feel better when they are upset, anxious, or angry. Think about the ones that you use, and then write in the answers to the questions.

Play Music

What music (songs or groups) do you like to listen to?

_____

_____

_____

How does this kind of music make you feel?

_____

_____

_____

What one song makes you feel happy? _____

What song would you listen to if you wanted to do something that is difficult for you (like study for a hard test)?

_____

_____

_____

_____

Exercise

What kind of exercise do you like to do?

_____

_____

How does it make you feel after you exercise?

_____

_____

Is there one kind of exercise/activity that you do that always makes you feel good about yourself?

_____

_____

Is there any kind of exercise that makes you feel worse than when you started?

_____

_____

With whom do you like to exercise?

_____

_____

Talk to a Friend or an Adult

Who is an adult that you can count on to help you feel better?

_____

_____

_____

Who is another child that you can count on to help you feel better?

_____

_____

_____

What might prevent you from talking to someone when you are upset?

_____

_____

_____

Can you think of a time that you talked to someone about a problem and you felt better?

_____

_____

_____

Play with a Special Toy or Do a Hobby

What is something you like to do that you never get tired of?

_____

_____

_____

Why do you enjoy it?

_____

_____

_____

Do you think that this is something you can do to help control your difficult feelings?

_____

_____

_____

What other activities do you like to do that make you feel calm or relaxed?

_____

_____

_____

...And More to Do!

Describe some times when you wished you could have changed your feelings.

_____

_____

_____

Many people have a hard time changing their angry feelings. How would you do this?

_____

_____

_____

Barry was sad because his grandfather died. Even after a month, he cried every night when he went to bed. What would you advise him to do?

_____

_____

_____

Cory was mad because his mother had remarried. He didn't like his stepfather at all. What would you advise Cory to do?

_____

_____

_____

_____

Activity 13   Being More Cooperative

> ## *For You to Know*
>
> Being more cooperative will make your life much easier and more fun, too. Everyone appreciates cooperative kids.

Some things can't be done without cooperation.

- You can't seesaw by yourself.

- If you want to lift a heavy or large object, you will need help.

- If you can't reach something on a high shelf, someone will have to help you get it down.

Other things can be done without cooperation, but they are more difficult and less fun to do by yourself.

- If you want to play catch, you could throw a ball against a wall, but it is more fun to play with someone else.

- You can take a photograph of yourself with a digital camera, but it is much easier to ask someone else for help.

- You can play a few games, like solitaire, by yourself, but most games are played with other people.

Being cooperative means that you are willing to help out other people when they ask and even when they don't ask. When you have a cooperative attitude, people appreciate it, and they will want to help you out, too.

Your challenge: Find ways to be more cooperative with others. See if you notice a difference in the way that they treat you.

For You to Do

How would it help to be cooperative in the following three situations? Draw a picture of what the child in each situation could do to be more cooperative.

Sara's mom had a hard day at work. She said, "I have a headache and I really don't feel like fixing dinner." What could Sara do to help her mom?

Shannon left her homework on the kitchen table. Her friend Riley wanted to help Shannon out. What could Riley do?

Aaron's father said he was going to clean out the garage. What could Aaron do to help?

...And More to Do!

What are some ways that you could be more cooperative around the house?

_____

_____

_____

What are some ways that you could be more cooperative at school?

_____

_____

_____

What are some ways that you could be more cooperative with your friends?

_____

_____

_____

What do you think is the most important reason that you should be more cooperative?

_____

_____

_____

For You to Know

It is important to be a helpful person. If you can find a way to be helpful to others every day, you will feel good about yourself and others.

In this assignment, I want you to learn one simple fact: People like helpful people.

Being a helpful person is really simple. It is also really important.

On the next page, there are five simple things you can do to be helpful. Your assignment is to write five more things. Then, tomorrow, try to do all ten things!

If you can do five to seven things to be more helpful, you get a "B," if you can do eight to ten things to be helpful, you get an "A." If you do more than ten things to be helpful, you get an "A+."

Your challenge: Constantly look for ways that you can be helpful to others.

For You to Do

Make a check mark in the box when you have done each thing.

☐   Hold the door for someone.

☐   Help someone carry something.

☐   Offer to get something for someone who is seated.

☐   Do an extra chore.

☐   Share something of yours.

Now add five more things that you can do.

☐   _____

☐   _____

☐   _____

☐   _____

☐   _____

...And More to Do!

Who is someone that you think is very helpful? _____

Who is someone you know who is well liked? Describe them.

_____

_____

_____

Describe something that happened when you were helpful to another child.

_____

_____

_____

Describe something that happened when you were helpful to a parent.

_____

_____

_____

Describe something that happened when you were helpful to a teacher.

_____

_____

_____

Activity 15   Setting Positive Goals

For You to Know

If you want to change something about yourself, it is easier if you set a goal and work toward it.

Nobody is perfect, but I'm sure that your parents and teachers want you to try to do some things differently. They may lecture you or punish you or put you on some kind of reward program, but I also know that you will change the way you act only when you want to.

When you want to change your behavior, it is easier if you begin with a goal.

For example, your goal might be to:

- Do your homework on time.

- Do more sit-ups.

- Learn a new spelling word every day.

You probably noticed that these are all positive behaviors that your parents and teachers would like you to improve. Do you perhaps have some of your own positive things that you would like to improve? These could be your goals, too.

Your challenge: To decide on a goal that is important to you.

For You to Do

It is important to set goals at school, but it is not always easy. Your goal in this activity is to get through the maze of school work without crossing any lines. Do you think you can do it?

...And More to Do!

Write down four positive goals.

_____

_____

_____

_____

Which of these goals is most important? _____

Write down how you are going to work toward this goal.

_____

_____

_____

What do you think might keep you from working on your goal?

_____

_____

_____

How will you know when you have accomplished your goal?

_____

_____

_____

For You to Know

It is important to be able to be patient. People who are patient are usually more successful in the things that they do.

Patience is an important virtue, a personal quality that almost everyone values. But even though it is important to know how to be patient, no one really teaches this to kids.

Instead, our culture gives kids the impression that everything should be quicker and quicker.

- We have meals that can be made in the microwave in a few minutes.

- We have high-speed Internet access and ever faster computers.

- We have tens of thousands of fast-food restaurants across the country.

- We have overnight delivery for things that we order, so that we can purchase the things that we want and get them in less than a day.

- We have cell phones so that we never have to wait a minute to get to a phone.

All of these things are fine, except that they make it harder to wait and be patient when there is really no other choice.

Kids aren't the only ones that can have a problem being patient. I'm sure you have seen adults who get frustrated and act badly even though being patient is the only thing that will help.

Your challenge: Be patient when you are frustrated. Take a deep breath and let it out slowly. Keep calm and things will go better.

For You to Do

How would it help to be more patient in the following three situations?

Draw a picture of what the child in each situation could do to be more cooperative.

Frank hated waiting for his mom while she shopped. What could he do to keep himself from getting bored?

Kelly wanted a video game that all of his friends owned. His parents said that he could have it for his birthday, but that was six months away.   What could he do?

Trent hated math. It took him hours to do his math homework. He felt like just throwing it all in the garbage can. What could he do to help himself be less frustrated?

...And More to Do!

Can you think of a recent time when you showed you were patient?

_____

_____

_____

Can you think of a type of job where people have to really be patient? What would happen if they weren't patient?

_____

_____

_____

Who is a person who is very patient with you? Ask them if they are ever impatient.

_____

_____

_____

Give an example of a situation where you need to learn to be more patient. How will you become more patient?

_____

_____

_____

Activity 17   Making Compromises

For You to Know

If you don't learn how to make compromises, you will always have problems with other people. No one likes people who always have to get their own way. In a compromise, everyone gets something of what they want, but they don't get everything that they want.

Making compromises is something that all kids have to learn, but I guarantee that when you learn how to make good compromises you will be happier. When you learn to make compromises, you will have fewer fights and arguments. When you learn to make compromises, you will have more friends. When you learn to make good compromises, adults will be more likely to respect your opinions. It is important to remember that you can't compromise with adults about everything. Adults make the rules, and most of the time you have to follow them. You can offer to make compromises with your parents and teachers about some things, but you must be willing to accept that there are some things that adults will not compromise on.

Here are some examples of when adults compromised with kids.

- Jason wanted to play baseball, but his mother wanted him to finish his book report. They agreed that he would finish the report after playing baseball for two hours.

- Annie wanted her mom to buy her new sneakers. Her mom said that she would pay for half the cost of the sneakers if Annie would earn money to pay for the other half.

Here are some examples of when adults will not compromise with kids.

- Henry wanted to ride his bike without a helmet, just around the neighborhood. His father said that he had to wear his helmet every time he got on his bike.

- Sarah felt that she didn't have to brush her teeth every day. She suggested that she brush her teeth every other day. Her mother said, "Forget about it."

If an adult won't accept your compromise, be polite and accept "no" for an answer. That way they will be more likely to accept a compromise at another time.

For You to Do

Read this story about friends who settled an argument by compromising.

The Three Friends

Once upon a time there were three friends, Emmy, Michael, and Kayla. One Saturday they were all at Emmy's house trying to decide what to do.

"I think we should play kickball," Emmy said first.

"No," said Michael, "I don't want to play kickball. We always play kickball. I want to play basketball today."

"But I don't like basketball," Emmy said. "You just want to play basketball because you're tall. But I'm short and I'm no good at basketball. Kickball is much more fun for everybody."

"I don't feel like playing ball," said Kayla. "I want to stay inside and watch cartoons. Besides, it looks like it is going to rain."

"No, it doesn't," said Emmy.

"Yes, it does," said Kayla.

"Does not," said Emmy.

"Does too," said Kayla.

"Stop arguing!" shouted Michael. "You're giving me a headache! Let's do something that we all can agree on."

"Okay," said Emmy, feeling a little bad that she was arguing with her friend.

"Okay," said Kayla, who was also feeling bad.

"So now what do we do?" said Michael.

"I know," said Emmy. "We'll compromise. My mom said a compromise is all of us agreeing on a plan that will make everybody happy."

"Well, why don't we just take turns deciding what we'll do," said Kayla.

"That's a good idea," said Michael, "but who will get to go first?"

"I know," said Emmy, "we can write down our names on pieces of paper and crumple them up. Then Kayla can shut her eyes and pick one piece of paper at a time. The first name picked gets to choose what to do this Saturday, the next person gets to pick what to do next week, and the third person gets to pick what to do the week after that."

"Okay," said Kayla, "that's a good idea."

"Okay," said Michael, "that's a good idea."

"Okay," said Emmy, "then I guess we have a plan."

The moral: When you disagree with someone, you can work out a plan so that everyone can be happy, even though everyone does not get exactly what they want.

...And More to Do!

Can you think of a good compromise that you made recently? What happened?

_____

_____

_____

Can you think of an argument that you had with a parent or teacher that could have been avoided with a compromise?

_____

_____

_____

Who do you know at school who is good at creating a compromise? Give an example of a compromise he/she suggested.

_____

_____

_____

Do you know of an adult who will always suggest a compromise rather than have an argument? Give an example of a compromise he/she suggested.

_____

_____

_____

Activity 18   Making a Commitment to Change

For You to Know

When you make a commitment to changing, it is easier to change your behavior.

Do you know what a contract is? A contract is a written agreement that says you will do something important. Putting what you will do in writing is different from just saying that you will do something. When you agree to a contract and then you sign it, you are making an important promise to do something. Breaking your contract is a serious thing.

Here are some examples of contracts that adults make:

- A marriage contract

- A lease for a car or a place to live

- A loan, which is an agreement to pay back money

- A partnership contract, which is an agreement on how people will work together in business

All of these are adult contracts, and if people break these contracts they often have to go to court.

Children often have a "behavioral contract," which is not a legal contract, but it is still important. Sometimes there are negative consequences (punishments) if you break your contract and positive consequences (rewards) if you keep your contract.

Your challenge: With an adult, decide on an important behavior that you want to change, and make a contract that promises you will do what you say.

For You to Do

My Contract

With_____
        Name Of Adult

I, _____
            Name Of Child

WILL _____
            Required Effort

_____
    Child's Signature

_____
    Adult's Signature

© ParentStore.Com   *Permission is granted to reproduce this chart for personal or professional use.

...And More to Do!

Why is it important to honor a contract?

_____

_____

_____

Why do you think that written contracts are more important than just saying that you will do something?

_____

_____

_____

Sometimes people want to change behaviors that have become "bad habits." What are some bad habits that you think you should change?

_____

_____

_____

Who do you know who has changed a bad habit? Ask them how they did it, and write their answer here.

_____

_____

_____

Changing Unhelpful Patterns

For You to Know

People get into patterns of doing the same thing over and over again, even if what they are doing is causing a problem.

Many times, if you do just one thing differently, anything at all, you can break the pattern and stop the problem.

For example, Tyrone hated to go to school. He didn't have any friends in his class, and he thought that his teacher didn't like him. Every morning he would have an argument with his mother about going to school. He would yell at her, and she would yell at him. Every day, he went to school in a bad mood, and things got worse from there.

Now think of the things that Tyrone could have done differently:

- He could have stopped arguing with his mom (it didn't do any good anyway).

- He could have found something about school that he liked and looked forward to.

- He could have made one friend in school to hang out with.

- He could have talked with his mother about his problems at school instead of just arguing with her.

Your challenge: Think of one thing you can do differently when you are unhappy about things.

For You to Do

Tyrone said that he hated to go to school, and he argued about going every day. What could he do differently?

_____

_____

_____

_____

Frank complained that nobody wanted to play with him. What could he do differently?

_____

_____

_____

_____

Jason liked to tease the little kids to make everyone laugh. What could he do differently to get attention?

_____

_____

_____

_____

...And More to Do!

Can you think of a behavior pattern (something unpleasant that happens over and over again) that you need to change?

_____

_____

_____

A professional basketball player might break his foul shot into steps and analyze each step if he is having a problem. Can you break your behavior pattern into steps?

_____

_____

_____

Sometimes people find it hard to do something different. What aspect of your behavior do you think would be very hard for you to change?

_____

_____

_____

Do you know someone who finds it easy to change his/her behavior? These people are considered to be flexible. Would you like to be more flexible about your behavior? How can you do this?

_____

_____

_____

For You to Know

You can change your behavior quicker when you keep track of your progress.

Many children feel that adults are always trying to control them. Adults make the rules, and they enforce them in ways that kids don't like.

But you can control your own behavior and be your own boss! It begins by learning to measure your progress toward your goals. You can do this by self-monitoring what you do.

Self-monitoring means paying attention to your own behavior and keeping track of it. You have probably heard of a hall monitor. A hall monitor pays attention to what happens in the school hallways between classes and reports problems to the teacher. When you self-monitor, you keep track of the things you do wrong and the things you do right, and report them to yourself!

You may already keep track of your behavior by self-monitoring. For example, if you want to run faster you may practice running every day for an hour. Then you monitor your speed by using a stopwatch.

The card on the next page will help you self-monitor your behavior. The first thing you will do is write in a behavior goal. A behavior goal is something that you want to improve about yourself. For example:

- Do my homework without being reminded.

- Keep my room clean.

- Get up on time for school.

Your challenge: Keep track of your progress in achieving all of your goals.

For You to Do

Make copies of the card below and use one card for each day of the week. Write in a behavior goal that you want to change. Then, at the end of the day, circle the number that best describes your behavior, with 1 = Poor, and 5 = Great.

After one week, add up your score on all seven cards. Any score above 21 is a good start. Then use the cards for another week, and see if you can improve your score!

Today's Date _____

_____

My Goal

1 2 3 4 5

...And More to Do!

Why do you think it is important to control your behavior?

_____

_____

_____

Is there an area in particular that you would like to improve?

_____

_____

_____

Would you describe yourself as a "motivated person" or an "unmotivated person"? Explain your answer.

_____

_____

_____

_____

Who do you know that has a lot of self-discipline? Why did you choose that person?

_____

_____

_____

For You to Know

Kids often complain that they have to follow many rules, but rules have a purpose. When you show that you respect rules, you eventually get more responsibility in making your own decisions. When you show that you don't respect rules, you get into trouble and usually you end up with adults making even more rules.

Everyone has to follow rules; not just kids, but adults too.

Imagine what would happen if there were no rules about how to drive.

Imagine what would happen if there were no rules about how to behave toward others.

Imagine what would happen if there were no rules in a football or baseball game.

There might be certain rules in your life that you understand and other ones that you think are unfair. Even if you think a rule is unfair, you still have to follow it. Then, when you show that you respect the rule, you might be able to negotiate a compromise that you think is more reasonable.

Your challenge: Respect the rules, even when you don't like them. Find positive ways to change the things in your life that you don't like.

For You to Do

Write down the ten most important rules in your life. These can be adult rules or rules that you make for yourself.

My Rules

①
2.
3.
4.
5.
6.
7.
8.
9.
⑩

...And More to Do!

If you made the rules for adults, what is the first rule you would make?

_____

_____

_____

What is the one rule that you think is totally unfair? How would you change it?

_____

_____

_____

Have you ever tried to negotiate a change in a rule? What happened? What could you have done differently?

_____

_____

_____

What is a rule that you don't like, but that you see is still a good rule to have?

_____

_____

_____

For You to Know

A lot of people have a hard time keeping their tempers. Even adults may yell and carry on when they are frustrated or upset. But yelling and losing your temper doesn't help. There are better ways to deal with your anger.

On the next page you'll find a game that can help you learn to keep your temper.

Take five coins and toss each one, trying to land it in the "cool down circles." Each circle shows good ways that you can deal with your anger. If you can do this, you get the number of points indicated in the circle, but only after you demonstrate the technique. If a coin lands on one of the angry faces, you get points taken away.

If you get five points or more, you win!

For You to Do

...And More to Do!

What is something that makes you angry?

_____

_____

_____

Would you say that you get angry more or less than other people?

_____

_____

_____

What is a good way to express your anger?

_____

_____

_____

What are some bad ways that people express their anger?

_____

_____

_____

The Loud and Nasty Voice

For You to Know

It is important to control the tone and volume of your voice when you talk to others. When you raise your voice or when you use a nasty tone of voice, people will not want to do what you ask. When you use a pleasant voice, people will be more likely to do what you ask.

When you were young, your teachers or your parents might have reminded you to use an "indoor voice" when you were too loud. When you were running around outside, you could use your "outdoor voice."

But the volume of your voice is just one of the ways that your voice affects other people. Your voice tone is also very important in how people think about you and treat you. People communicate many things in their voice tone. With a pleasant voice tone, they communicate interest, concern, and caring. With an unpleasant voice tone, they communicate anger, disrespect, and an uncaring attitude.

In this activity, you will learn to think about your voice tone and what it communicates to others, particularly adults.

Your challenge: Think about what you say to others and the way you say it. If you find yourself using a nasty and unpleasant tone of voice, take a deep breath and try to say things with a neutral or pleasant tone.

For You to Do

Practice saying these sentences in a calm, quiet, and pleasant voice. Say each sentence five times. Start by saying each with a "nasty tone," and then make it more pleasant each time you say it.

Don't talk in a fake or overly sweet voice. Using that kind of voice makes people feel that you are insincere, and it is almost as bad as speaking in a nasty voice.

If you have a tape recorder, make a recording of your voice and play it back so that you can hear how you sound to other people.

"I don't want to do my homework now. May I do it later?"

"I don't like spinach. May I have something else?"

"I got a 'D' on my test, and I'm in a bad mood."

"I want to stay up and watch a movie on TV. May I?"

"Are you mad at me?"

...And More to Do!

When do you think it is particularly important to speak in a pleasant tone of voice?

_____

_____

_____

What should you do if someone speaks in a nasty tone of voice to you?

_____

_____

_____

Can you think of a character on TV or in the movies who uses a nasty tone of voice all of the time?

_____

_____

_____

Is there anytime when it is okay to use a nasty or unpleasant tone of voice?

_____

_____

_____

For You to Know

When you do something good for someone else each day, you will also feel good about yourself.

What do you think it means to be good? Here are some of the things that adults think of as good behavior:

- Respecting rules.

- Being kind to others.

- Studying hard.

- Doing chores and homework without asking.

- Being polite.

- Being considerate of others.

Do these behaviors describe you? Are there other behaviors that you would call "good behaviors"?

In this activity, you will make an effort to do one good behavior each day, for one week. Write it down so that you will remember it. You can make extra copies of the picture of the diary on the next page, or you can just use your own paper. Make sure that you don't skip even one day.

At the end of the week, read about what you have done and decide if you can continue your Good Behavior Diary for a longer period of time (like forever).

For You to Do

My
Good Behavior Diary

...And More to Do!

Of the people you know at school, who always has good behavior? Describe something that they did that makes you feel this way.

_____

_____

_____

Some kids make fun of others who are "too good." Why do you think that they do this?

_____

_____

_____

Why do you think that it is important to write down the good deeds that you do?

_____

_____

_____

Many people think that television and movies are bad influences on kids. What do you think?

_____

_____

_____

> ## *For You to Know*
>
> The words that you use play a big part in determining your attitude and your feelings.

Words are very powerful.

Words can hurt people's feelings.
Words can cheer people up.

Curse words can get you into big trouble.
An apology can help correct a mistake.

Mean words will make you unpopular.
Kind words will usually make people like you.

Disrespectful words will get adults angry at you.
Respectful words will make adults treat you with respect.

Think about people who use a lot of negative words to you or around you.

How do you feel when they use these words? What do you do?

Your challenge: Use more positive words when you speak to people, and see if they change the way that they react to you.

When you catch yourself saying negative words, immediately try and make a positive statement.

For You to Do

Put each of these positive words into a sentence as if you were talking to another person. Try to create sentences that will make other people respond well to you.

For example:

Nice: You look nice today.

Okay: Okay, I'll do it right away!

Great: _____

_____

Awesome: _____

_____

Sure: _____

_____

Right: _____

_____

Best: _____

_____

Yes: _____

_____

Help: _____

_____

...And More to Do!

Describe a situation when you said negative or mean things. What happened?

_____

_____

_____

Describe a situation when you would normally say something mean but you could say something nice.

_____

_____

_____

Who is one person that you think would find it helpful to use more positive words? What will you say? What do you think that they will say or do?

_____

_____

_____

Who among your friends or acquaintances uses respectful words with adults? Why do you think that they do this?

_____

_____

_____

Being Positive with Your Friends

For You to Know

It's important to say positive things to your friends and treat them in a positive manner. If you often criticize them or argue with them, soon they won't be your friends.

Almost everyone agrees that it is important to have friends, but some kids have more friends than others. Kids who have many friends know that treating people with respect and consideration is the best way to make and keep friends.

Some kids think that it is cool to be sarcastic and to tease other kids. They may make mean jokes or call other kids names. Even when it is done in fun, calling people names will get you into trouble and make it hard to keep friends.

In this exercise, you should work on learning the difference between positive and negative ways to treat other kids.

Your challenge: Treat everyone with respect and positive words, and notice how they treat you back.

For You to Do

Write in examples of positive things that are being said in blue. Write in examples of negative things that are being said in red.

...And More to Do!

Why do you think that kids tease each other?

_____

_____

_____

What does it mean to be sarcastic? Give an example of how a kid might be sarcastic.

_____

_____

_____

What could you do if you said something that hurt a friend's feelings, besides apologize?

_____

_____

_____

Can you think of a time that you regret something that you said to a friend?

_____

_____

_____

For You to Know

There are different kinds of lies and some lies are more serious than others. If you lie to people a lot of the time, they won't trust you.

You have probably been told that it is always important to be truthful and that you should never ever tell a lie. But you may also realize that even adults don't always tell the truth. Maybe you have heard your parents say something that wasn't true, like calling in to their work to say that they were sick, but they really wanted to spend the day with you. Sometimes people even tell a lie to spare someone's feelings. For example, you might say to someone, "I like your new shoes," just to make them feel good, even though you don't really like the way the shoes look.

Even though few people tell the truth 100% of the time, there are some times when you must always tell the truth.

- You must always tell the truth to your parents and teachers.

- You must always tell the truth when someone might get hurt.

- You must always tell the truth about something you did that was wrong.

- You must always tell the truth about rules in your home or school.

For You to Do

Read this story about a boy who learns to tell the truth.

Donald, the Mad Scientist

Once upon a time there was a brainy boy named Donald. His dream was to become a scientist. He loved to talk about science and about his future as a great scientist.

On Monday, he would talk about his plans to study insects. On Tuesday, he planned to become an astronaut. On Wednesday, he talked about volcanoes. On Thursday, he discussed his future studies of sharks and dolphins. And on Friday, he bragged that he would design a robot. He said, "I'll make a robot that will do my homework, play video games with me, tell jokes, and tie my shoes."

The boys and girls at Donald's school were very interested in a robot that could do all of these things. That afternoon, the teacher announced that each student must complete a project for the school science fair. The next Friday, everyone in the class would have to present their projects to the class and to discuss what they had learned.

Donald's friend Manuel said to him after school, "You should build your robot for the science fair!"

"I don't know," said Donald, who secretly worried that he did not know how to build a robot.

Then his friend Mark said, "It's perfect. Why wouldn't you build your robot? Unless you don't know how …"

"Of course I know how," said Donald quickly.

That weekend, Donald thought and thought about how to build a robot. He looked around his room to find useful items: rubber bands, paper clips, paper towel rolls, glue. He drew plans in blue pencil, and he read a book about robots. Donald learned that it took many, many years for scientists to learn how to build robots. He was too embarrassed to tell the other kids at school that he might not be able to build a robot after all.

All the next week at school, the other boys and girls asked, "How's the robot today? Does it work? Has it tied your shoes yet?"

"Yes, yes," said Donald every day. "The robot is amazing. It does everything." Donald immediately regretted telling this lie. The truth was that Donald could not make a robot that would walk or talk, no matter how hard he tried.

Finally it was the day before the science fair, and Donald was in his room. He was looking at his sad little robot. Donald had used a cereal box for the body, garbage ties for the antennae, hangers for its arms and legs, plastic cups for its eyes. Donald was very, very tired from working so hard, and he was afraid to go to school the next day. Everyone would see that the robot was a disaster and that he was no scientist.

The next morning he begged his mother to let him stay home from school. "Look!" he said, pointing at the lopsided robot. One of its arms had fallen off overnight. Donald felt miserable — everybody was expecting a walking, talking robot, and he had lied to them.

His mother said, "Tell me what's bothering you, Donald."

"I told everyone the robot could walk and talk, so I really don't want to go to school," Donald said. "Everyone thinks I'm going to be a great scientist when I grow up, but they won't believe me once they see that!" The other arm fell off the sad-looking robot. Donald started crying.

His mother reminded him that he should not have lied to his friends in the first place. "I know," said Donald, wishing he had just told his friends that building a robot was harder than he thought.

"Great scientists, painters, teachers, carpenters, all have to learn by practice," his mother said. "It's okay if things are not perfect, as long as you try hard and learn something along the way. There is nothing to be ashamed about, except lying. It's much better to admit that you were bragging than to lie about what you have done. Lying always makes things worse."

Donald went to school with his robot. He stood up in front of the class and propped the robot up on the desk. He said, "This is my robot. It doesn't really do all the things that I wanted it to do. I got carried away with my imagination. And that's the truth."

The moral: It's wonderful to have a great imagination, but you shouldn't lie about what you can do. Being caught in a lie is embarrassing, but telling the truth will usually make things right again.

...And More to Do!

What do you think is the most common reason that kids lie? Give an example.

_____

_____

_____

What do you think is the most common reason that adults lie? Give an example.

_____

_____

_____

Do you think it is possible to always tell the truth, no matter what happens?

_____

_____

_____

What is the worst lie that a kid could tell?

_____

_____

_____

For You to Know

When you don't tell the truth you can get into serious trouble and you may find that you are alone and unhappy. No one will trust someone who lies all of the time, and when people don't trust you, it is harder for them to care about you.

You may have heard the fable about the boy who cried wolf. He thought it was funny to pretend that a wolf was coming and to see his family and the people in his village run out to fight the wolf. He pretended that a wolf was coming over and over again, and so people just started to ignore him. Then one day, a wolf really did come to the village. But when the boy cried out for people to protect him from the wolf, the people in the village just ignored him. You probably know what happened next. The boy was carried off by the wolf, never to be seen again.

In real life, the things that happen when you lie are not usually so dramatic, but sometimes they are pretty bad.

I know one boy who lied to his parents about getting his report card. He told them that his teacher wasn't giving a report card for several months, but he had hidden his actual report card under his bed. The report card had all failing grades because the boy had not done any homework since the beginning of school. (He told his parents that his teacher did not believe in homework, which was also a lie). But he forgot that report cards had to be signed by parents and returned to school. When the report card wasn't returned, the boy's teacher called his parents and scheduled a meeting. When the boy's parents found out that he had gotten poor grades and that he had lied, they were most upset about his lying. They did not let him watch TV for three months, and they made him do his homework at the kitchen table in front of them for two hours a day.

Your challenge: Think about the consequences of your words and actions.

For You to Do

Below you will find different lies that kids told. Write down what you think will be the consequence to each one of these lies:

The Lie

"I already fed the dog."

What could happen?

_____

_____

The Lie

"Yes, I brushed my teeth well."

What could happen?

_____

_____

The Lie

"I don't have a spelling quiz this week."

What could happen?

_____

_____

The Lie

"Marty said that he thinks you are stupid."

What could happen?

_____

_____

...And More to Do!

What is the worst lie that you ever heard of?

_____

_____

_____

Have you ever told a lie, but nothing bad happened?

_____

_____

_____

Do you think that something may have happened that you just didn't know about? What could it be?

_____

_____

_____

Susan told little lies all of the time. She told her friends that she went to Disney World on vacation, but she really didn't. She told her piano teacher that she practiced every night, but she usually practiced only once a week. What do you think might happen to Susan as she grows up?

_____

_____

_____

Activity 29

Avoiding the Bad Influences of Others

For You to Know

Sometimes kids you know may do things that they shouldn't, like tease other kids, steal something, or even damage things that belong to others. You might have a friend or even a group of friends that wants you to do things that you know are wrong.

Other kids may put a lot of pressure on you to do things that are wrong. They may call you a "baby" or tease you in other ways. They may say that they don't want to hang around with you anymore. They may try and make you feel that there is something wrong with you if you don't do what they are doing.

Even though it may be hard, you should still not do things that are wrong.

Here are some things to remember when someone wants you to do something that you know is wrong:

- Talk to a grownup about what is right and wrong.

- Believe in yourself and what you think is right.

- Stand up for your rights, no matter what anyone says to you.

- Don't let the desire to be popular change your decisions.

- Find friends you can have fun with who enjoy the things that you like to do.

Your challenge: Learn how to stand up to pressure from your friends.

Avoiding the Bad Influences of Others

For You to Do

Draw a picture of another child trying to get you to do something that is wrong. What is that child trying to get you to do?

Now draw a picture showing how you will solve this problem.

...And More to Do!

Do you know kids who do things that are wrong? Why do they do these things?

_____

_____

_____

Sydney's friends wanted her to try a sip of beer. They said that one sip would not hurt. What would you say if you were Sydney?

_____

_____

_____

Mathew marked on his desk with permanent markers. He handed you a marker and told you to mark up your desk too. What should you do?

_____

_____

_____

With whom can you talk if you are worried about doing something that is wrong just to please your friends?

_____

_____

_____

For You to Know

Taking things that belong to others is very serious. Stealing is always wrong, whether you are caught or not. Kids won't be put in jail for doing these things, but they will face serious punishments.

Just as there are different kinds of lies, there are different levels of what belongs to others.

Taking a cookie from the cabinet when you've been told not to do it is wrong. Your parents have rules that must be followed, and you can be punished if you break these rules.

Taking a toy from another child's cubby at school is very wrong and will make that child unhappy. It can also get you punished at school or even suspended. Stealing candy from a store is considered even more serious and can get you in trouble with the police. Children who steal things all of the time go to court, and a judge will decide what should be done to help them stop stealing.

There are different reasons that kids steal things, but it is always wrong and kids will almost always be punished for stealing.

Your challenge: Make a promise to yourself that you will never steal things—and keep your promise!

For You to Do

Make up a story about a boy who stole a video game so that he could give it to his best friend for his birthday. Make sure that you include the lesson that the boy learned.

The Story

_____

_____

_____

_____

_____

_____

_____

_____

The Lesson

_____

_____

_____

...And More to Do!

Babies don't know that it is wrong to take things that belong to others. When do you think a child is old enough to know that it is wrong to steal? Who told you that it is wrong to steal?

_____

_____

_____

Have you ever taken something that belonged to someone else? What happened?

_____

_____

_____

There are some grownups who take things that belong to others. If they are caught, they go to jail. They are called thieves. Why do you think that grownups steal things?

_____

_____

_____

If you took something that belonged to a friend and he or she found out about it, what would you do to make things right?

_____

_____

_____

For You to Know

Many kids tease each other. Sometimes teasing is meant to be fun, and sometimes it is meant to be hurtful, but nobody really likes to be teased.

There are many ways that kids tease each other. Sometimes kids call each other names, like: "You're a geek."

Sometimes kids say things that aren't true, like: "Your mother is as fat as a house."

Sometimes kids say things that are true, but are not nice, like: "You know that you're the worst reader in the class, don't you?"

Sometimes kids just make silly faces or gestures to annoy other kids. I'm sure that you've seen that before.

I've never met anyone who likes to be teased. Teasing is mean and hurtful. If you tease other kids, there might be some people who think you are funny, but most people will see that you are just being mean.

You may find that it is hard to stop teasing. Maybe you tease your little sister because she annoys you. Maybe you tease other kids at school because they tease you. It doesn't matter why you used to tease other kids as long as you stop doing it. This activity should help.

Your challenge: Make a promise to yourself that you will stop teasing others— and keep it!

For You to Do

In each situation, think of what you can do instead of teasing.

The Situation

A kid in your class calls you a name.

What would you do?

_____

_____

The Situation

Your friends are making fun of a new kid.

What would you do?

_____

_____

The Situation

In school you are wearing clothes that don't match.

What would you do?

_____

_____

The Situation

You want to be in a group of kids, but they spend a lot of time making fun of other kids.

What would you do?

_____

_____

The Situation

Your friends are having a joke-telling contest, but all of the jokes make fun of other people.

What would you do?

_____

_____

The Situation

You are really angry at another child, and you feel like saying something mean to him or her.

What would you do?

_____

_____

...And More to Do!

Can you think of any time that it is okay to tease other kids?

_____

_____

_____

Do you ever tease your parents? What do they say or do?

_____

_____

_____

Do your parents ever tease you? What do they do? What do you say to them?

_____

_____

_____

Why do you think so many kids tease each other?

_____

_____

_____

Activity 32　　　　Making New Friends

> ## *For You to Know*
>
> It is important to know how to make new friends. The best way to begin is by finding out something that you have in common.

Everyone likes kids who are friendly. When you say hello to people that you meet and look them in the eyes, you give off the message that you are someone people will want to be with.

Making new friends can be harder for some children than others. You probably know some children who seem to have lots of friends and other children who have only a few friends or no friends at all. The good news is that you can learn how to make friends; and when you practice what you learn, making friends will become easier to do. When you learn how to make friends, you will never be lonely again!

Here are some things to remember about making new friends:

- Find something that you have in common.

- Talk about what interests you.

- Ask questions about the other person.

- Show respect for kids who have different opinions.

- Accept that you can't always have your way, and be willing to compromise.

Your challenge: Use the different things that you have learned in this workbook to help you make and keep good friends. It can take a little to work to have good friends, but it is worth it.

For You to Do

Look at this group of kids.
Circle the one kid that you would talk to first.
Put a box around the one that you think is the leader of the group.

Arnold   Berta   Carrie   Debra   Eve

What activity would you suggest that you think these kids would enjoy?

_____

_____

Close your eyes and see if you can remember the names of each of these kids.

...And More to Do!

What are some of the things you like best about your friends?

_____

_____

_____

Why do you think that some children are more popular than others?

_____

_____

_____

Why do you think that it is hard for some children to make friends but easy for others?
Do you think it is the way that they were raised, or were they just born friendly?

_____

_____

_____

Harry moved to a new neighborhood and started going to a new school. Name some
things that other kids could do to make him feel welcome.

_____

_____

_____

For You to Know

It is important to always show respect to adults, including your parents, your teachers, the adults who work in your school, the adults who work in stores … any adults at all.

Many children are disrespectful to adults.

- They talk back.

- They don't listen when adults talk.

- They don't do what adults ask them to do.

- They may use bad language or even call adults names.

Of course you should be respectful to kids as well as adults, but it is different. If you are disrespectful to other kids, you will soon find that you don't have many friends. But if you are disrespectful to adults, you will be punished and you will be in constant trouble.

When you are respectful to adults, you will find that everything in life gets easier. Adults treat you better. Your parents are proud of you. Your teachers give you more help and show that they like you in many ways.

Here are some of the ways that you can show respect to adults.

- Always use good manners.

- Always listen to an adult when he/she is speaking.

- Don't interrupt.

- Be helpful to adults.

- Do what you are told to do with a pleasant attitude.

Your challenge: Always think about how you can be respectful to others.

For You to Do

Read this story about a boy who learns to talk to others respectfully.

Barry Badder's Backtalk

Once upon a time there was a boy named Barry Badder who talked back to his parents. When he talked back to adults, they would get very mad. Sometimes they would yell. Sometimes they would send him to time-out. Sometimes they would take away his toys or send him to bed. But all of these things just made Barry Badder madder. The more he was punished, the more Barry would talk back to his parents.

The situation became worse and worse. Barry's parents blamed each other for Barry's bad behavior and backtalk. It became so bad that the Badder family would fight all the time. They wondered, "What could make the Badder family better?"

Finally, Barry's grandmother suggested they see a counselor. Barry's grandmother was a counselor herself, and she said that she was sure things would get better once they learned better ways to talk to each other. Barry's grandmother said that she knew a counselor who would see them the very next day.

Mr. and Mrs. Badder were glad to go to someone who could help their family treat each other better. They put Barry in the car, and they all went to see Dr. Betty Banner.

Dr. Banner said, "Barry, it is important that you respect your parents and not talk back to them. Mr. and Mrs. Badder, you need to show Barry a good example, and be respectful to each other, too."

"Now, I'm going to give you a simple technique to help you say what is on your mind. Simply say, "I feel _____ (whatever you are feeling), because _____ (say the reason without blaming anyone), and I want _____ (say what you want)."

"That's all there is to it," Dr. Banner explained. "Now you try it. Barry, you go first."

Barry said, "I feel angry when you put me in time-out because that's not fair, and I want you to stop doing that."

Barry's mother said, "I feel better when you tell me what is bothering you, because I think we can work things out. And I want you to tell me when you are upset."

Barry's father said, "I feel we are making some progress, because nobody is yelling, and I want to do anything I can to help make Barry learn to be respectful and happier."

After their meeting, the Badder family started to feel much better. They practiced talking to each other with respect the way Dr. Banner had taught them. They still disagreed sometimes, but they found themselves fighting much less. Barry rarely got punished, which was certainly much better for him.

The moral: Talking back is disrespectful. You should always be polite and considerate when talking to anyone. Saying what you feel, what you want, and why you want it will usually help things get better.

...And More to Do!

Can you think of a time when it is particularly important to be respectful to an adult?

_____

_____

_____

Why do you think that some kids are disrespectful, even though it gets them into trouble?

_____

_____

_____

What would happen if you were disrespectful to a police officer?

_____

_____

_____

Can you think of a situation where you should have been more respectful to an adult? What might have happened if you had been more respectful?

_____

_____

_____

Developing Your Empathy

For You to Know

When you have empathy it means that you know how another person feels. When you are sensitive to the feelings of other people, you will develop more fulfilling relationships. Caring about others is one of the most important of all human emotions.

People are born with the ability to feel empathy toward others. Even babies will hear another baby cry and cry too. It is almost as if they are saying, "I know that you feel bad, and although I don't know why or what to do, I'll cry too!"

Empathy is the reason that people try and help each other. For example, if you heard that a friend's grandmother had died, you would understand that they must be very sad, and you might try to make them feel better.

Empathy is also the reason that we give to charities. We know that many people around the world live in hunger or don't even have electricity in their homes, and we want to help them because we understand how hard that must be.

Being empathetic is the opposite of being selfish or self-centered. It is a trait that everyone admires, and it will help you get along with everyone in your life.

It's not at all hard to be empathetic. Even babies can do it!

Your challenge: Whenever you have a serious talk with someone, try and think about their point of view and what they are feeling.

For You to Do

Write your answers to the questions about how others might feel.

Jonathon told you a secret about his family. What might happen if you told the secret to someone else?

_____

_____

_____

_____

Samuel made a joke out of flunking his spelling test. Why would he do this? How do you think he really feels?

_____

_____

_____

_____

Martha's teacher looks worried. What do you think she could be worried about?

_____

_____

_____

_____

...And More to Do!

Who do you know that has a lot of empathy? Why did you choose that person?

_____

_____

_____

Can you think of something that you did recently that showed your concern about the feelings of someone else?

_____

_____

_____

Why do you think that people who are empathetic are well liked?

_____

_____

_____

If a friend of yours was very sad, what would you do to cheer him or her up?

_____

_____

_____

For You to Know

Virtually every school in the United States has a "no touching" rule. This means that you don't touch other children for any reason.

Touching other children at school is never a good idea, but some kids do it anyway.

- Kids punch.

- Kids push.

- Kids kick.

- Kids pinch.

- Kids poke.

- Kids try to trip other kids.

- Kids may even touch the private areas of other children.

When kids touch each other in inappropriate ways, it is very serious. They can get suspended from school or even expelled.

Of course, there are good ways to touch other people, too.

- You can hug a close friend or family member.

- You can shake hands to say hello.

- You can put your arm around someone you are close to, to comfort them.

I'm sure that you know the difference between good touches and touches that are wrong. This is a very important rule to remember and follow.

Your challenge: Be aware of rules about touching other people, and follow them.

For You to Do

In the boxes below, draw three rules about touching. Write the rule in the space below your drawing.

You should always keep your hands to yourself in line.

Example

...And More to Do!

Ronald liked to wrestle with his friends at recess. But his teacher said to stop or he would be in trouble. Why would this be a problem?

_____

_____

_____

Sara wanted Sean to be her boyfriend. One day she kissed him in the coat closet, and their teacher saw them. They both got suspended from school for three days. Do you think that this was fair? Why or why not?

_____

_____

_____

Daniel hit Patrick, because Patrick tripped him. But Daniel is the one who got in trouble! Do you think that this was fair?

_____

_____

_____

What happens in your school if you hit or push someone on the playground?

_____

_____

_____

What Do You Dream About?

For You to Know

You can make many of your dreams and wishes come true if you try hard enough.

Everyone has dreams about the kind of person they want to be. Some kids dream that they will be a rock star. Other kids dream that they will be a great baseball player. Some kids dream about the things that they want for themselves or for others.

Some kids work hard to achieve their dreams. They may not get exactly what they dream about, but they do achieve great things. Even if you have problems in your life, you can achieve great things. Many famous and successful people were poor when they were children, had serious family problems, or had a very hard time in school. But these problems didn't stop them. They found a way to make their dreams come true. Did you know that even Albert Einstein, one of the most brilliant scientists that ever lived, had a hard time in school when he was young? Did you know that Walt Disney, who had the idea for Mickey Mouse, and Disney World, and many great things, was very poor when he was young and didn't do well in school?

But some kids think that just wishing and dreaming is enough. They may daydream about all the great things they will do or have, but they don't try to make these things happen. What do you think usually happens to these kids?

Your challenge: Think about what you really want for yourself or for others and how you can achieve your dreams.

For You to Do

Write down what you wish for yourself in the box below. Then write three things you can do to make your wish come true.

Your Wish

_____

...And More to Do!

If you won a million dollars in a contest, how would you spend it?

_____

_____

_____

Suppose you won a million dollars, but the contest rules said that you had to spend all of the money on other people. What would you do?

_____

_____

_____

If you had super powers, what would they be? How would you use these powers to help others?

_____

_____

_____

What "powers" do you have in real life? How can you use these powers to help others?

_____

_____

_____

Activity 37

Letting Others Know How Great You Are

For You to Know

Everyone has faults and everyone has good qualities. Sometimes people look more at our faults and our problems than they do at our positive qualities. You need to let people know about your good qualities through your words and your actions.

It seems to be human nature that people find it easier to see our faults rather than our good qualities.

For example, James was a very smart boy and an exceptional basketball player. He had a good sense of humor and a lot of friends. But he didn't like to do writing assignments. He told his mother, "Writing gives me a headache." But his mother just said, "Too bad, everyone has to learn how to write."

James would argue about doing his homework every night, and his mother would be mad at him more and more. Then he would be mad at her more and more. His mother was still aware of his good qualities, but she only paid attention to the problem that James had with doing his homework.

You might be thinking that James's mother is a bad person for treating him this way, but the truth is that James has to take responsibility for this problem, too. James should work on doing his writing assignments without complaining, and he should also remind his mother of his positive qualities.

Your challenge: Work on your faults, but also let people know of your many great qualities.

For You to Do

Top 10 Things
I Want You To Know About Me!

1.

2.

3.

4.

5.

6.

7.

8.

9.

10.

...And More to Do!

Describe yourself, using ten positive words.

_____   _____

_____   _____

_____   _____

_____   _____

_____   _____

What is something really great that you did in the last month?

_____

_____

_____

Who do you think really knows you well and appreciates you?

_____

_____

Who do you think really needs to know about your good qualities?

_____

_____

_____

What Do You Want to Achieve?

For You to Know

You have more control over your life than you might realize.
You can make a plan to achieve the things that you want.

I bet that you have been asked, "What do you want to be when you grow up?" many times.

I also bet that your answer to this question changes all of the time.

You may not know exactly what kind of job you want to have when you grow up, but you may know the kind of person you want to be and some things that you want to accomplish. Which of these statements describe what you want?

- I want to have a lot of friends.

- I want to travel all over the world.

- I want to live in a big house and have lots of stuff.

- I want to be someone that people look up to and admire.

- I want to have a lot of children.

- I want to do things that I can be proud of.

- I want to be a leader and have power over lots of people.

- I want to do things with animals.

- I want to do, make, or invent great things.

The statements that you checked are based on your values, what you think is important in life. Knowing your values will help shape your decisions as well as your actions. Knowing what you want will help you get it.

Your challenge: Think about the things that you want to achieve and what you have to do to become the kind of person you want to be.

For You to Do

Fill this bookshelf with trophies and awards you will achieve as you grow up. Make sure that you write what each one is for.

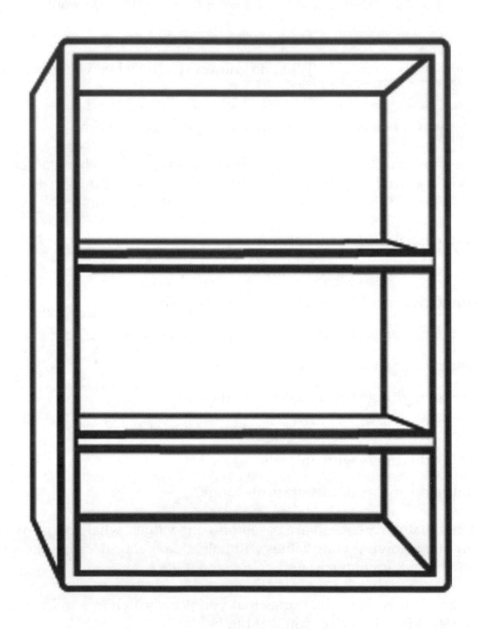

What Do You Want to Achieve?

...And More to Do!

What would you say is the greatest achievement you have accomplished so far in your life?

_____

_____

_____

What special talents do you have that will help you achieve new things in your life?

_____

_____

_____

What famous person would you like to be like when you grow up? Explain your answer.

_____

_____

_____

What nonfamous person would you like to be like when you grow up? Explain your answer.

_____

_____

_____

For You to Know

Changing your behavior can be hard, but it is easier if there is an adult that you can turn to for guidance.

There are many adults who can help you change your behavior in addition to the other things that you learned in this workbook. These include:

- Parents

- Teachers

- Counselors

- Grandparents and other family members

- Coaches

- Clergy

- Mentors

Most kids find it easier to talk to some people than to others. Sometimes, parents are the best people to help you, but other times you might get the most help from someone you don't know that well, like a counselor. Counselors (and sometimes teachers and other adults, too) have been trained to help kids with problems, and they know just what to do.

The first thing you will have to do is to trust the people that are trying to help you. They may not always tell you exactly what you want to hear, but they can guide you into making choices that will make you both happy and successful.

Your challenge: Find at least one adult that you can turn to when you need help with a problem.

For You to Do

Fill in the pictures below of two people you can go to for help when you need it. Then draw a picture of yourself after you've gotten the help you need.

My Best Friend

My Best Friend

...*And More to Do!*

Why do you think that some people don't like to ask for help, even when they need it?

_____

_____

_____

What is a problem that you could use help with?

_____

_____

_____

Who do you think can best help you with that problem?

_____

_____

_____

When will you ask for the help that you need?

_____

_____

_____

Lawrence E. Shapiro, Ph.D., is a nationally recognized child psychologist who is known for his innovative play-oriented techniques. He has written over two dozen books and created over forty therapeutic games. Shapiro is founder of the Childswork/ Childsplay catalog and publishing company, a leading distributor of psychologically oriented toys and games. He is author of numerous books, including *How to Raise a Child with a High EQ: A Parents' Guide to Emotional Intelligence* and *The Secret Language of Children*.

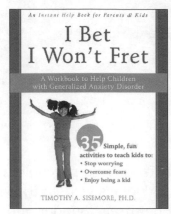
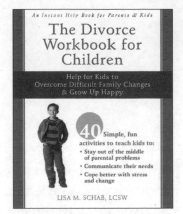